THE ULTIMATE 101 GUIDE TO FREELANCING

© **Pd John**

Copyright

All rights reserved, it is not permitted to copy, reprint or duplicate this book without the permission of the author.

Major Prophet PD John
P.O. BOX 4016
Mwanza - Tanzania
Phone number:
+255 762 415 790/ +255 759 204 744
Yohanayona3@gmail.com
www.hl centre.info

ISBN : 9798329166125
First edition ©2024.
Imprint: Independently published

Chief Editor:
Josia pd John
josiajohn735@gmail.com
Dar es salaam - Tanzania
Tel: +255 758588127/ +255 693522834

The Ultimate 101 Guide to Freelancing

Dedication:

To all the freelance warriors who blaze their own trail, defy the odds, and fearlessly pursue their passions, this book is dedicated to you. May THE ULTIMATE 101 GUIDE TO FREELANCING serve as your compass, your mentor, and your constant companion on this exhilarating journey. Here's to endless opportunities, boundless creativity, and the unwavering belief that anything is possible when you dare to dream big. This is for you.

Preface:

Welcome to The ***Ultimate 101 Guide to Freelancing!*** Whether you're a seasoned professional looking to embark on a new career path or someone just starting out in the world of freelancing, this book is here to provide you with the essential knowledge, strategies, and tools to succeed in the ever-growing freelance economy.

In today's fast-paced and rapidly changing world, the traditional 9-to-5 job may no longer offer the flexibility, fulfillment, and opportunities we desire. Freelancing, on the other hand, allows us to take control of our careers, work on our terms, and embrace the endless possibilities of a digital marketplace.

This guide aims to be your go-to resource, offering a comprehensive roadmap for launching and growing a successful freelancing business. From understanding the freelance landscape and identifying your skills and passion to setting up your business, finding clients, and managing contracts, we'll cover it all. Additionally, we'll explore the crucial aspects of marketing yourself as a freelancer, balancing work and lifestyle, and taking care of your physical and mental well-being.

Drawing on my own experiences as a freelancer and insights from successful freelancers across various industries, I've compiled this book to provide you with practical advice, useful tips, and real-life examples that will empower you to make informed decisions and navigate the freelancing world with confidence.

I firmly believe that freelancing is about more than just making a living; it's about creating a life that aligns with your passions, values, and aspirations. By embracing freelancing, you are taking a bold step towards designing a career that offers freedom, creativity, and personal fulfillment.

While this book offers a comprehensive foundation, it's important to remember that freelancing is a journey of continuous learning and growth. As technology evolves and trends shift, you'll need to adapt and refine your skills. The world of freelancing is ever-changing, and this guide is meant to serve as your companion along the way.

So, are you ready to embark on this exciting journey? Let's dive in and discover how you can turn your skills, passions, and dreams into a flourishing freelance business. Get ready to unleash your potential, embrace the freedom of freelancing, and create a life and career on your own terms.

Best wishes on your freelancing adventure!

Prophet PD John

Introduction:

In the modern age, the concept of freelancing has gained tremendous popularity, offering individuals the opportunity to break free from traditional employment and embrace a more flexible, independent work lifestyle. In this introduction, we will define freelancing, explore its historical roots, and highlight its significance in the contemporary economy. Additionally, we will discuss the purpose and goals of this book, as well as the inclusion of biblical scriptures that provide insight and guidance for freelancers.

1. Definition and Overview of Freelancing:

Freelancing refers to a self-employed individual offering services to multiple clients on a contractual basis. Unlike traditional employment, freelancers have the freedom to choose the projects they work on, set their rates, and determine their own schedules. This allows for greater autonomy and the ability to pursue work that aligns with personal passions and skills.

2. Brief History of Freelancing and its Rise in Popularity:

While the concept of freelancing has been around for centuries, it has witnessed a significant surge in popularity in recent years. In biblical times, individuals such as artists, craftsmen, and merchants were akin to freelancers, taking on commissions and selling their goods or services to earn a living. Examples from the Bible, such as the skilled craftsmanship of Bezalel and Oholiab in Exodus 31:1-11, highlight the ancient roots of freelancing.

In the modern era, digital advancements and globalization have facilitated the growth of freelancing. Online platforms and marketplaces enable freelancers to connect with clients from around the world, transcending geographical limitations. This shift in the working landscape has fueled the rise of the gig economy and contributed to the increasing popularity of freelancing.

3. Importance and Benefits of Freelancing in the Modern Economy:

Freelancing plays a crucial role in today's economy, providing benefits not only for individuals but also for businesses and society as a whole. The benefits of freelancing include:

- Flexibility: Freelancers have the freedom to choose their working hours, allowing them to pursue other personal commitments and passions.

- Variety: Freelancers can engage in diverse projects, honing their skills and broadening their professional experiences.

- Autonomy: Freelancers have control over their work, utilizing their creativity and expertise to deliver high-quality outcomes.

- Economic Growth: Freelancing contributes to economic growth by fostering entrepreneurship, innovation, and job creation.

- Enhanced Work-Life Balance: Freelancers often have the ability to strike a harmonious balance between work and personal life, reducing stress and promoting overall well-being.

4. Goal and Purpose of the Book:

The goal of this book is to provide aspiring freelancers with a comprehensive guide that equips them with the knowledge, strategies, and tools needed to navigate the freelancing world successfully. By incorporating biblical scriptures, we aim to offer guidance and wisdom from a spiritual perspective, illustrating how principles from the Bible can be applied to the unique challenges and opportunities faced by freelancers.

Throughout the book, examples will be shared to demonstrate how biblical principles, such as stewardship, integrity, and the pursuit of excellence, can shape a freelancer's mindset and approach to their work. These references will serve as sources of inspiration and guidance, reminding freelancers that their work is not only a means of earning a living but also an opportunity to live out their faith and make an impact on the world.

As we embark on this journey through the world of freelancing, let us seek wisdom from timeless biblical teachings and practical insights, empowering us to thrive in our freelancing careers while staying true to our values and purpose.

Prophet PD John

Table of Contents

Copyright 1

Dedication: 2

Preface:..2

Introduction: 5

Table of Contents 9

Chapter 1: Getting Started with Freelancing 11

1.1 Understanding the Freelance Landscape 11

1.1.1 Types of Freelancing Industries and Opportunities 12

1.2 Identifying Your Skills and Passion 16

1.3 Crafting Your Freelancing Vision 22

Chapter 2: Setting Up Your Freelancing Business 27

2.1 Legal and Financial Considerations 27

Testimony: 30

2.2 Creating an Effective Freelance Brand 31

2.3 Crafting a Winning Freelancing Proposal . 36

Testimony: 40

Chapter 3: Finding Clients and Marketing Your Services 41

3.1 Identifying Potential Clients and Target Market 41

3.2 Networking and Building Relationships ... 45

3.3 Effective Marketing Strategies for Freelancers 50

Chapter 4: Navigating Freelancing Contracts and Negotiations 55

4.1 Understanding the Importance of Contracts 55

Personal Testimony: 57

4.2 Negotiation Techniques for Freelancers 61

4.3 Managing Client Relationships 66

Chapter 5: Balancing Work and Lifestyle as a Freelancer 72

5.1 Time Management and Productivity Techniques 72

5.2 Financial Planning and Budgeting 77

5.3 Self-Care and Avoiding Burnout 82

Personal Testimony: 85

Conclusion: 86

Chapter 1:

Getting Started with Freelancing

1.1 Understanding the Freelance Landscape

Freelancing is a diverse and expanding field, offering a wide range of opportunities across various industries. In this chapter, we will explore the different types of freelancing industries, discuss the pros and cons of freelancing, and delve into the decision-making process of freelancing as a side gig versus a full-time career.

1.1.1 Types of Freelancing Industries and Opportunities

Freelancing encompasses a vast array of industries, providing individuals with the flexibility to pursue their interests and leverage their skills. Some common freelance industries include:

1. Creative Industries: This includes fields such as graphic design, writing, photography, illustration, and videography. Freelancers in these industries often work on projects such as designing logos, creating marketing materials, writing articles, capturing images, or producing videos.

2. IT and Programming: With the constant evolution of technology, freelancers with programming and IT skills are in high demand. From web development and mobile app creation to software engineering and cybersecurity, freelance opportunities in this sector are plentiful.

3. Marketing and Advertising: Freelancers in marketing and advertising help businesses reach their target audiences, develop effective strategies, and create compelling content. This can involve tasks like social media management, content writing, SEO optimization, and digital advertising campaigns.

4. Consulting and Professional Services: Consultants offer specialized expertise in various fields, such as management, finance, HR, or legal services. Freelancing in this sector involves providing advice, analysis, and solutions to clients.

5. Teaching and Training: Online education has become increasingly popular, creating opportunities for freelancers to offer courses, tutoring services, or specialized training in areas like language learning, coding, fitness, or personal development.

These are just a few examples, but the freelance landscape is vast and constantly evolving. It is essential to research and identify the industries that align with your skills, passion, and market demand.

1.1.2 Pros and Cons of Freelancing

Before diving into freelancing, it is crucial to understand the advantages and disadvantages it offers:

Pros:

- Flexibility: As a freelancer, you have the freedom to choose your working hours, projects, and clients. This allows for a more adaptable schedule, which can be especially beneficial for individuals with other commitments or those seeking work-life balance.

- Variety: Freelancing brings diversity to your work life. Each project and client is unique, providing opportunities for personal and professional growth. The ability to work on different projects allows you to expand your skill set and experience different industries.

- Income Potential: Freelancers have the potential to earn more compared to traditional employment due to higher hourly rates, the ability to negotiate project fees, and the possibility of taking on multiple clients simultaneously.

Cons:

- Irregular Income: Freelancing often means variable income, as projects can be sporadic and clients may pay on different schedules. This requires careful financial planning and the ability to manage cash flow during lean periods.

- Self Employment Responsibilities: As a freelancer, you are responsible for handling all aspects of your business, including marketing, administration, and tax obligations. It is crucial to understand and manage these responsibilities effectively.

- Lack of Stability: Unlike a steady job, freelancing does not offer the security of a consistent paycheck or employee benefits such as health insurance or retirement plans. Freelancers must create their own safety nets and plan for periods of uncertainty.

1.1.3 Freelancing as a Side Gig vs. Full-time Career

One of the decisions individuals need to make when starting freelancing is whether to pursue it as a side gig or a full-time career. Both options have their merits:

- Side Gig: Freelancing as a side gig involves taking on freelance projects alongside a full-time job or other commitments. This allows individuals to test the waters, build a client base, and generate additional income while maintaining the security of a steady paycheck. However, juggling multiple responsibilities may require careful time

1.2 Identifying Your Skills and Passion

In order to succeed as a freelancer, it is crucial to identify and leverage your skills, experiences, and passions. In this section, we will explore strategies for assessing your abilities, discovering your unique talents, and identifying potential niches for your freelancing business.

1.2.1 Assessing Your Skills, Experiences, and Interests

Start by conducting a thorough self-assessment of your skills, experiences, and interests. Consider your past work experiences, education, and any specialized training or certifications you have obtained. Reflect on the tasks and projects you have enjoyed and excelled at, as well as the areas where you have received positive feedback or recognition.

Ask yourself the following questions:

- What are my core skills and strengths?

- What tasks or activities do I enjoy the most?

- What experiences and expertise do I bring to the table?

- Are there any areas where I have received positive feedback or recognition?

- What type of work aligns with my values and interests?

Consider taking online assessments or personality tests that can provide insights into your strengths, preferences, and potential areas of focus. This can help you gain a better understanding of your unique abilities and identify areas where you can excel as a freelancer.

1.2.2 Discovering Your Unique Talents and Strengths

Identifying your unique talents and strengths is crucial in setting yourself apart from the competition and attracting clients. Your talents and strengths are the skills or qualities that come naturally to you and set you apart from others.

Consider the following approaches in discovering your unique talents and strengths:

- Reflect on past successes: Think about the times when you achieved outstanding results or made a significant impact. What skills or strengths did you utilize to achieve those accomplishments?

- Seek feedback: Ask trusted friends, family, colleagues, or mentors for their insights on your strengths and unique qualities. They may provide valuable perspectives that you may not have considered.

- Experiment and explore: Engage in different activities or projects to explore new skills and discover what you enjoy and excel at. This can help uncover hidden talents and passions that can be leveraged in your freelancing career.

- Utilize online platforms: Take advantage of online platforms such as LinkedIn, GitHub, or Behance to showcase your work and receive feedback from professionals in your field. This can help you gain insights into your strengths and areas for improvement.

1.2.3 Identifying Potential Niches for Your Freelancing Business

Once you have assessed your skills, experiences, and passions, it is time to identify potential niches for your freelancing business. A niche is a specific area or specialization within an industry where you can focus your services. By targeting a niche, you can position yourself as an expert in a particular field, making it easier to attract clients and stand out in a crowded market.

Consider the following steps in identifying your potential niche:

1. Research the market: Conduct thorough market research to understand the demand for various services within your industry. Identify gaps or underserved areas that align with your skills and interests.

2. Analyze your competition: Study your competition within your potential niches. Identify

their strengths, weaknesses, and areas where you can differentiate yourself.

3. Assess your target audience: Determine who your ideal clients are within your chosen niche. Understand their needs, pain points, and preferences. This will help you tailor your services and marketing efforts to attract and retain clients.

4. Evaluate profitability: Consider the financial viability and potential profitability of your chosen niche. Assess factors such as market demand, potential client budgets, and the pricing models typically used in your niche.

Remember, choosing a niche does not mean limiting yourself. As you gain experience and grow your business, you can expand your services or target additional niches. Starting with a focused approach allows you to establish a strong foundation and build credibility within a specific area.

By assessing your skills, discovering your unique talents,

1.3 Crafting Your Freelancing Vision

Setting a clear vision is crucial for success as a freelancer. In this section, we will explore strategies for setting realistic goals and expectations, defining your values and principles, and developing a long-term vision for your freelancing career.

1.3.1 Setting Realistic Goals and Expectations

When starting your freelancing journey, it is important to set realistic goals and expectations. This will help you stay motivated, focused, and on track towards achieving your desired outcomes. Consider the following steps:

1. Identify your objectives: Clearly define what you want to achieve through freelancing. It could be financial goals, work-life balance, personal growth, or pursuing a passion.

2. Break it down: Dividing your objectives into smaller, manageable goals will make them more achievable. Set specific, measurable, attainable, relevant, and time-bound (SMART) goals that align with your overall vision.

3. Consider external factors: Take into account market conditions, competition, and the demands of your chosen industry. Understanding these factors will help you set realistic expectations and adjust your goals accordingly.

4. Regularly review and adjust: Periodically review your goals and assess your progress. Be open to adjusting your goals based on changes in the market, personal circumstances, or new opportunities that arise.

Remember to set goals that challenge you without overwhelming you. Finding a balance between ambition and feasibility is key to maintaining motivation and avoiding burnout.

1.3.2 Defining Your Values and Principles as a Freelancer

Your values and principles serve as a compass guiding your actions and decisions as a freelancer. Clearly defining them will help you build a strong foundation and attract clients who align with your beliefs. Consider the following steps:

1. Reflect on your values: Identify the core principles and values that guide your personal and professional life. Consider what is truly important to you, such as integrity, creativity, collaboration, or social impact.

2. Align with your work: Determine how you can incorporate your values into your freelancing career. For example, if environmental sustainability is

important to you, you might choose to work with clients or projects that share this commitment.

3. Communicate your values: Clearly articulate your values on your website, social media profiles, and in client interactions. This will attract clients who align with your values and help build a strong professional reputation.

By aligning your freelancing business with your values, you will find greater fulfillment and satisfaction in your work, attracting clients who appreciate and support your principles.

1.3.3 Developing a Long-Term Vision for Your Freelancing Career

Having a long-term vision is essential for planning and guiding your freelancing career. It allows you to set a direction and make strategic decisions that align with your desired outcome. Consider the following steps:

1. Envision your future: Visualize where you want to be in 5, 10, or 15 years as a freelancer. Imagine the type of work you will be doing, the clients you will serve, and the impact you will make.

2. Identify milestones: Break down your long-term vision into smaller milestones or achievements that will lead you closer to your ultimate goal. These milestones act as stepping stones and provide a sense of progress along the way.

3. Create an action plan: Develop a concrete plan that outlines the steps and resources needed to achieve each milestone. Set deadlines and hold yourself accountable to stay on track.

4. Stay adaptable: While having a long-term vision is important, it's essential to remain adaptable and open to new opportunities or changes in the market. Be willing to adjust your vision as needed to stay relevant and seize emerging opportunities.

Your long-term vision will serve as a guiding light, helping you make decisions that align with your ultimate goals and ensuring that your freelancing career progresses in the direction you desire.

By setting realistic goals, defining your values and principles, and developing a long-term vision

Chapter 2:

Setting Up Your Freelancing Business

2.1 Legal and Financial Considerations

When starting a freelancing business, it is important to address legal and financial considerations to ensure a smooth and compliant operation. This section will discuss key aspects such as registering your business name, taxes, licenses, setting up a separate business bank account, and establishing payment methods and pricing strategies.

2.1.1 Registering your Business Name, Taxes, and Licenses

One of the first steps in setting up your freelancing business is registering your business name. Choose a name that reflects your brand and is memorable for clients. Check with your local government to verify any specific requirements for registering a business name in your jurisdiction.

Next, consider your tax obligations. Consult with a tax professional or research the tax laws in your country to understand how to meet your tax obligations as a freelancer. This may include registering for a tax identification number, keeping track of your income and expenses, and filing taxes on time.

Additionally, depending on your industry or the services you provide, you may need specific licenses or permits. Research the regulations and requirements in your field to ensure that you operate legally and avoid any potential issues in the future.

2.1.2 Setting up a Separate Business Bank Account

Separating your personal and business finances is crucial for managing your freelancing business effectively. Opening a separate business bank account allows you to keep track of your income and expenses easily, simplifies tax preparation, and presents a more professional image to clients.

Contact various banks to compare their business account offerings and choose one that suits your needs. Provide the necessary documents, such as your business registration, tax ID, and identification, to complete the account opening process. Use this account solely for business-related transactions and avoid mixing personal and business funds.

2.1.3 Establishing Payment Methods and Pricing Strategies

Determining how you will receive payments and setting your pricing strategy is crucial for ensuring the financial success of your freelancing business. Consider the following factors:

Payment methods: Decide which payment methods you will offer to clients, such as bank transfers, PayPal, or credit card payments. Make sure to select methods that are secure, convenient for clients, and align with your financial goals.

Pricing strategy: Determine how you will set your prices. Consider factors such as your experience, expertise, market rates, and competition. Research industry standards and consider offering different pricing packages or options to cater to various client needs.

Testimony:

"As a freeluncer, I learned the importance of addressing legal and financial considerations early on in my business journey. Registering my business name and understanding my tax obligations allowed me to operate legally and avoid any potential issues in the long run. Setting up a separate business bank account was a game-changer for managing my finances efficiently and

presenting a professional image to my clients. Lastly, establishing payment methods and pricing strategies made the financial aspect of freelancing much smoother. I was able to offer convenient payment options to my clients and set competitive prices that reflected the value of my services. By taking these steps, I created a strong foundation for my freelance business, ensuring financial stability and compliance with legal requirements."

2.2 Creating an Effective Freelance Brand

Building a strong brand is essential for establishing your freelancing business and attracting clients. This section will explore key strategies for defining your personal brand identity, establishing a professional online presence, and showcasing your work through a portfolio.

2.2.1 Defining your Personal Brand Identity

Your personal brand is a reflection of who you are as a freelancer, what you stand for, and the unique value you offer to clients. Consider the following steps to define your brand identity:

1. Identify your target audience: Determine the specific group of clients you want to serve. Understand their needs, pain points, and preferences to tailor your brand messaging to resonate with them.

2. Define your unique value proposition: Identify the unique skills, expertise, or perspective you bring to your freelance work. This will differentiate you from competitors and attract clients who value what you have to offer.

3. Craft your brand message: Develop a compelling and concise brand message that communicates your value proposition and resonates with your target audience. This message should be consistent across all your marketing materials and communication channels.

4. Embrace authenticity: Be true to yourself and your values. Authenticity builds trust with clients and sets the foundation for long-lasting relationships.

2.2.2 Establishing a Professional Online Presence

In today's digital age, having a professional online presence is essential for freelancers to showcase their skills and connect with potential clients. Consider the following strategies:

1. Create a professional website: Build a website that showcases your services, portfolio, testimonials, and contact information. Make sure your website is visually appealing, easy to navigate, and mobile-friendly.

2. Leverage social media: Choose platforms that align with your target audience and engage with them regularly. Share valuable content, engage with

industry peers, and promote your services to build credibility and visibility.

3. Optimize your online profiles: Ensure your professional profiles on platforms like LinkedIn, Behance, or Upwork accurately reflect your brand identity and highlight your skills and experience. Use professional headshots and write compelling summaries that captivate potential clients.

4. Develop a consistent brand voice: Use a consistent tone, style, and language across all your online channels to reinforce your brand identity and make a memorable impression on clients.

2.2.3 Building a Portfolio and Showcasing your Work

A well-curated portfolio is essential for demonstrating your capabilities and attracting clients. Consider the following tips:

1. Highlight your best work: Select a range of projects that showcase your skills and expertise. Choose projects that are relevant to your target audience and demonstrate your ability to meet their needs.

2. Use professional presentation: Present your work in a visually appealing and organized manner. Include project descriptions, objectives, and outcomes to provide context for potential clients.

3. Collect testimonials and feedback: Reach out to satisfied clients and ask for testimonials or feedback. Display these on your website or portfolio to build trust and social proof among potential clients.

4. Keep your portfolio updated: Continuously add new projects to showcase your latest work and demonstrate growth and innovation to potential clients.

By defining your personal brand identity, establishing a professional online presence, and building a portfolio that showcases your best work, you will position yourself as a reputable and desirable freelancer in your field.

2.3 Crafting a Winning Freelancing Proposal

To secure freelance projects successfully, it is essential to master the art of crafting a winning proposal. This section will delve into understanding client needs and expectations, structuring a comprehensive proposal, and creating compelling samples and case studies.

2.3.1 Understanding Client Needs and Expectations

Before you begin crafting a proposal, take the time to understand your client's needs and expectations. This will allow you to tailor your proposal to align with their specific requirements. Consider the following steps:

1. Research the client: Familiarize yourself with the client's business, industry, and target audience. This will help you understand their pain points and how you can provide value.

2. Clarify project details: Schedule a consultation or exchange messages with the client to gather all the necessary information about the project. Ask questions to gain a clear understanding of their goals, timeline, and budget.

3. Analyze the competition: Research your client's competitors to identify areas where you can offer unique insights or solutions. This will demonstrate your understanding of their industry and position you as a valuable partner.

2.3.2 Structuring a Comprehensive Proposal

A well-structured and organized proposal can make a significant difference in winning freelance projects. Consider the following components for an effective proposal:

1. Introduction: Begin by introducing yourself, briefly explaining your expertise, and expressing your understanding of the client's needs and goals.

2. Scope of work: Clearly outline the specific tasks, deliverables, and timelines associated with the project. Be as detailed as possible and ensure that your proposal aligns with the client's expectations.

3. Methodology and approach: Describe your approach to solving the client's problem or meeting their needs. Explain the steps you will take, the resources you will utilize, and any unique strategies you will employ.

4. Pricing and terms: Present a transparent breakdown of your fees and expenses. Provide

different pricing options, if applicable, and clearly outline the terms of payment and any additional fees or expenses that may arise during the project.

5. Expertise and credentials: Highlight your relevant experience, certifications, or qualifications that make you the ideal candidate for the project. Include case studies or testimonials to showcase your past success and client satisfaction.

2.3.3 Creating Compelling Samples and Case Studies

Including samples of your work or case studies in your proposal can greatly enhance its effectiveness. Consider the following strategies:

1. Select relevant samples: Choose samples that align closely with the client's project requirements. This will help the client visualize your capabilities and see how your work relates to their specific needs.

2. Provide context: In each sample or case study, provide a brief overview of the project objectives, challenges you faced, and the outcomes you achieved. Explain your role in the project and highlight key results or impact you made.

3. Customize your samples: Tailor your samples or case studies to reflect the client's industry or target audience. This will demonstrate your ability to adapt and provide solutions that resonate with their specific market.

Testimony:

"Crafting winning proposals has been a vital skill in my freelancing journey. By taking the time to understand client needs and aligning my proposals with their expectations, I have been able to secure exciting projects and forge lasting relationships with clients. Structuring a comprehensive proposal with clear scopes of work, pricing, and terms has allowed me to communicate effectively and establish trust and transparency.

Including compelling samples and case studies in my proposals has been a game-changer as it allowed clients to see the quality of my work and the results I have achieved. By combining these strategies, I have consistently stood out among competitors and won projects that have helped me grow my freelancing business.".

Chapter 3:

Finding Clients and Marketing Your Services

3.1 Identifying Potential Clients and Target Market

To grow your freelancing business, it is essential to identify potential clients and target the right market. This section will explore strategies for defining your ideal client profile, researching target industries and companies, and utilizing online platforms and marketplaces.

3.1.1 Defining your Ideal Client Profile

Defining your ideal client profile is crucial for effectively targeting your marketing efforts. Consider the following steps:

1. Analyze past clients: Review your previous clients and projects to identify common characteristics, such as industry, size of the company, location, or specific needs. This will give you insights into the types of clients you enjoy working with and who appreciate your services.

2. Determine pain points: Identify the specific pain points or problems that your services can solve for clients. This will narrow down your target market to those who are most likely to require and benefit from your expertise.

3. Research demographics and psychographics: Consider the demographics *(e.g., age, gender, income)* and psychographics *(e.g., interests, values, attitudes)* of your ideal clients. This will help you understand their motivations and tailor your marketing messages accordingly.

3.1.2 Researching Target Industries and Companies

Once you have defined your ideal client profile, conduct thorough research to identify target industries and companies that align with your expertise and goals. Consider the following strategies:

1. Industry analysis: Research different industry sectors and identify the ones where your skills and services are in demand. Look for trends, challenges, or opportunities within these industries that could benefit from your expertise.

2. Company research: Identify specific companies within your target industries that could potentially benefit from your services. Look for companies that align with your values, have a track record of outsourcing work, or have a demonstrated need for your skills.

3. Utilize online resources: Explore industry-specific websites, directories, and forums to gather insights about potential clients. Look for news, events, or discussions that indicate upcoming projects or opportunities.

3.1.3 Utilizing Online Platforms and Marketplaces

Online platforms and marketplaces can be powerful tools for finding clients and marketing your services. Consider the following strategies:

1. Create a strong online presence: Be active on platforms like LinkedIn, Twitter, and relevant industry forums. Share valuable content, engage with potential clients, and establish yourself as an expert in your field.

2. Utilize freelance marketplaces: Join popular freelance platforms such as Upwork, Freelancer, or Fiverr to showcase your services and connect with clients looking for freelancers. Optimize your

profile and portfolio to stand out from the competition.

3. Network and collaborate: Attend industry conferences, webinars, or networking events, both online and offline, to meet potential clients. Build relationships with other freelancers who may refer clients to you and consider collaboration opportunities.

By defining your ideal client profile, conducting thorough industry and company research, and utilizing online platforms and marketplaces, you will be able to effectively target your marketing efforts and find clients who are the best fit for your services.

3.2 Networking and Building Relationships

In addition to identifying potential clients and utilizing online platforms, networking and building relationships are key strategies for finding clients and marketing your services. This section will explore strategies for building a strong professional network, leveraging social media and LinkedIn for client acquisition, and attending industry events and conferences.

3.2.1 Building a Strong Professional Network

A strong professional network can open doors to new opportunities and referrals. Consider the following strategies for building and nurturing your network:

1. Connect with colleagues and industry peers: Reach out to colleagues, fellow freelancers, and professionals in your field. Attend networking events or join relevant professional associations to meet and connect with like-minded individuals.

2. Offer value and help others: Be proactive in offering assistance, sharing resources, or providing valuable insights to your network. This positions

you as a helpful and knowledgeable professional, increasing the likelihood of referrals and recommendations.

3. Maintain relationships: Regularly stay in touch with your network, whether through emails, phone calls, or meetings. Keep them updated on your work and achievements, and make an effort to support and promote their endeavors as well.

3.2.2 Leveraging Social Media and LinkedIn for Client Acquisition

Social media platforms, particularly LinkedIn, can be powerful tools for client acquisition. Consider the following strategies:

1. Optimize your profiles: Ensure that your social media profiles, particularly your LinkedIn profile, are complete, professional-looking, and highlight your skills and expertise. Include examples of your work, endorsements, and recommendations from previous clients.

2. Engage with relevant content: Seek out and engage with industry-specific content and discussions on social media platforms. Share your insights, ask thoughtful questions, and actively participate in conversations to increase your visibility and attract potential clients.

3. Reach out strategically: Use LinkedIn's advanced search feature to find potential clients based on industry, location, or job title. Personalize your connection requests or messages to demonstrate your genuine interest in working with them and how you can provide value.

3.2.3 Attending Industry Events and Conferences

Attending industry events and conferences provides opportunities to network, learn, and showcase your expertise. Consider the following strategies:

1. Research and select relevant events: Identify industry-specific events and conferences where your target clients are likely to attend. Look for opportunities to speak, present, or participate in panel discussions to increase your visibility.

2. Prepare and engage: Before attending an event, research the speakers, participants, and topics being discussed. Come prepared with business cards, elevator pitches, and thoughtful questions to engage with potential clients and industry professionals.

3. Follow up strategically: After attending an event, follow up with the contacts you made. Send personalized emails or LinkedIn messages, referencing your conversation and expressing your interest in further discussions or collaborations.

By building a strong professional network, leveraging social media and LinkedIn for client acquisition, and attending industry events and conferences, you can effectively expand your reach, connect with potential clients, and establish yourself as a trusted expert in your field. These strategies can lead to valuable collaborations and referrals, contributing to the growth of your freelancing business.

3.3 Effective Marketing Strategies for Freelancers

To successfully market your freelancing services, it is important to develop a marketing plan, create a personal brand story, and leverage content marketing and social media. This section will explore these strategies in detail.

3.3.1 Developing a Marketing Plan on a Budget

Even with a limited budget, you can create an effective marketing plan for your freelancing business. Consider the following steps:

1. Define your goals: Determine what you want to achieve with your marketing efforts. This could be

acquiring a certain number of clients, increasing brand awareness, or expanding into new markets.

2. Know your target audience: Understand the needs, challenges, and preferences of your target audience. This will help you tailor your marketing messages to resonate with them.

3. Identify marketing channels: Explore cost-effective marketing channels that will reach your target audience. This could include social media platforms, email marketing, content marketing, or networking events.

4. Develop a consistent brand identity: Make sure your brand identity, including your logo, website design, and language, is consistent across all marketing channels. This helps establish recognition and credibility.

5. Set a budget: Allocate a specific budget for marketing activities. Be strategic in how you spend

your money, focusing on high-impact tactics that align with your goals.

6. Monitor and analyze results: Regularly track the success of your marketing efforts. Use analytics tools to measure website traffic, social media engagement, and lead conversion rates. This data will inform future marketing decisions.

3.3.2 Creating a Personal Brand Story

Crafting a compelling personal brand story can differentiate you from your competitors and attract clients who resonate with your values and vision. Consider the following steps:

1. Understand your unique value proposition: Determine what sets you apart from other freelancers in your industry. Identify your specific skills, experience, or approach that will appeal to potential clients.

2. Define your brand personality: Consider the tone, language, and visual elements that reflect your brand's personality. This should align with your target audience and the clients you want to attract.

3. Craft your brand story: Develop a narrative that showcases your professional journey, expertise, and the problems you can solve for clients. Highlight your passion, unique experiences, and success stories to captivate your audience.

4. Tailor your messaging: Adapt your brand story to different marketing channels and target audiences. For example, your storytelling approach on your website could differ from the way you present yourself on social media.

3.3.3 Leveraging Content Marketing and Social Media

Content marketing and social media can be powerful tools for freelancers to showcase their expertise, attract clients, and build a strong online presence. Consider the following strategies:

1. Create valuable content: Develop blog posts, articles, videos, or infographics that provide valuable insights or solutions to common problems faced by your target audience. Focus on establishing yourself as an expert in your field.

2. Share content on social media: Promote your content through social media platforms where your target audience is active. Engage with your audience, respond to comments, and encourage them to share your content.

3. Build relationships through networking: Use social media platforms, such as LinkedIn and Twitter, to connect and engage with potential clients, industry influencers, and fellow freelancers. Join relevant groups or participate in Twitter chats to expand your network.

4. Show your expertise: Participate in online discussions, answer questions on forums or industry websites, and provide insightful comments on relevant blog posts. This demonstrates your expertise and can attract potential clients.

By developing a marketing plan on a budget, creating a personal brand story, and leveraging content marketing and social media, you can effectively market your freelancing services and attract the right clients. These strategies allow you to showcase your expertise, build credibility, and differentiate yourself in a competitive market.

Chapter 4:

Navigating Freelancing Contracts and Negotiations

4.1 Understanding the Importance of Contracts

Contracts are crucial for freelancers as they provide a solid foundation for working relationships, protect your rights and interests, and help prevent misunderstandings or disputes. This section will explore the reasons why contracts are crucial for freelancers, the key elements of a contract, and how to avoid common legal pitfalls. Additionally, we will include a personal testimony to highlight the significance of contracts in real-life situations.

4.1.1 Why Contracts are Crucial for Freelancers

Contracts play a vital role in freelancing for several reasons:

1. Clear expectations: Contracts outline the scope of work, deliverables, timelines, and payment terms, ensuring both you and your client are on the same page. This helps prevent misunderstandings and ensures clarity throughout the project.

2. Protecting your rights: Contracts typically include clauses relating to intellectual property rights, confidentiality, and liability limitations. By having these provisions in place, you can safeguard your work and limit your liability in case of any disputes or legal issues.

3. Establishing payment terms: Contracts specify the payment structure, such as project milestones, hourly rates, or fixed fees. This ensures that you are compensated fairly for your services and provides a basis for pursuing payment if issues arise.

4. Building trust and professionalism: Using contracts demonstrates professionalism and commitment to your clients. It instills confidence in your capabilities and shows that you take your work seriously.

Personal Testimony:

"As a freelance graphic designer, I learned the hard way about the importance of contracts. Early in my career, I took on a project without a formal contract, relying solely on verbal agreements and mutual understanding. Unfortunately, the client disputed the final deliverables and refused to pay the full amount we had agreed upon. Without a contract to rely on, I had no legal recourse and ended up losing both time and money.

Since that incident, I have always made sure to have a detailed contract in place for every project. Not only does it protect my rights, but it also sets clear expectations for both parties involved. Contracts have become an essential part of my freelancing process, helping me avoid potential conflicts and allowing me to focus on delivering quality work."

4.1.2 Key Elements of a Contract

When creating a contract as a freelancer, there are several key elements to include:

1. Parties involved: Clearly state the names and contact information of both you ***(the freelancer)*** and your client.

2. Scope of work: Define the specific services you will be providing, including the project objectives, deliverables, and any deadlines or milestones.

3. Payment terms: Specify the payment structure, such as the total fee, payment milestones, due dates, and any late payment penalties or interest charges.

4. Intellectual property rights: Clearly outline who will own the rights to the work created during the project. Consider including provisions for any licensing or usage rights needed by the client.

5. Confidentiality and non-disclosure: Include clauses that protect any confidential information shared during the project and prohibit the client from sharing or using that information without consent.

6. Termination clause: Establish conditions under which the contract can be terminated by either party, including notice periods or potential penalties.

7. Dispute resolution: Outline how potential disputes or issues will be resolved, such as through mediation, arbitration, or small claims court.

It is important to note that contracts should be tailored to the specific needs of each project and may require legal guidance to ensure they are comprehensive and enforceable.

4.1.3 Avoiding Common Legal Pitfalls

To avoid common legal pitfalls in freelancing contracts, consider the following tips:

1. Get professional advice: Consult with a lawyer or legal professional to draft or review your contract. They can ensure it complies with relevant laws and includes all necessary provisions.

2. Put it in writing: Always have a written contract rather than relying solely on verbal agreements. Written contracts provide

4.2 Negotiation Techniques for Freelancers

Negotiation skills are essential for freelancers to ensure fair compensation, maintain healthy client relationships, and establish professional boundaries. This section will explore various negotiation techniques specific to freelancing, including pricing strategies, handling client objections, and setting healthy boundaries and professional etiquette.

4.2.1 Pricing Strategies and Determining Rates

Determining your rates as a freelancer can be challenging, but it is crucial for sustaining a profitable business. Consider the following pricing strategies:

1. Market research: Conduct thorough research to understand the average rates charged by other freelancers in your industry and geographic location. This will provide a baseline for setting competitive rates.

2. Value-based pricing: Instead of solely basing your rates on time spent, consider the value you provide to clients. Focus on the outcomes, benefits, and impact your work will have on their business.

3. Tiered pricing: Offer different service packages at various price points to cater to different client budgets and needs. This allows you to showcase the value of your premium services while still accommodating clients with smaller budgets.

4. Consider your expenses: Take into account all your business costs, including overheads, taxes, and insurance, when determining your rates. Ensure that your rates are not only covering your time but also leaving room for profit.

4.2.2 Handling Client Objections and Negotiations

Negotiating with clients is a common occurrence in freelancing. Here are some techniques for handling objections and negotiations effectively:

1. Listen actively: When clients voice objections or concerns, listen carefully to understand their perspective. Be empathetic and show that you value their input.

2. Offer alternative solutions: Instead of dismissing objections outright, propose alternative solutions that address their concerns while still protecting your own interests.

3. Highlight your value: Clearly communicate the value and benefits your services bring to the client's business. Emphasize how your skills and expertise can solve their problems or achieve their goals.

4. Be firm and confident: While being open to negotiation, maintain confidence in your rates and abilities. Clearly articulate the reasons behind your pricing structure and the value you bring to the project.

5. Find common ground: Look for areas of agreement and build upon them. Focus on shared goals and finding win-win solutions that meet both your needs and the client's.

4.2.3 Setting Healthy Boundaries and Professional Etiquette

Maintaining healthy boundaries and demonstrating professional etiquette are essential in freelancing. Consider the following tips:

1. Set clear expectations: Clearly communicate your boundaries and limitations from the beginning of the client relationship. Establish guidelines for communication, availability, and project scope.

2. Respond promptly and professionally: Maintain open lines of communication, and respond to client inquiries or requests in a timely and professional manner. Prompt communication shows reliability and dedication to the project.

3. Practice assertiveness: Be respectful but firm when asserting your boundaries or negotiating terms. Clearly communicate your needs and requirements without compromising your professionalism.

4. Know when to say no: It's important to recognize when a project or client isn't the right fit for you. Saying no to potential projects that don't align with your skills, values, or availability is crucial for maintaining a healthy freelance business.

5. Be proactive in conflict resolution: If conflicts arise, address them promptly and professionally. Seek mutually beneficial solutions and prioritize maintaining positive client relationships whenever possible.

By implementing these negotiation techniques, freelancers can navigate pricing discussions, handle objections effectively, and foster healthier working relationships with clients. Remember, negotiation is a skill that improves with practice, so continually strive to refine your approach.

4.3 Managing Client Relationships

Effectively managing client relationships is crucial for freelancers to build a strong reputation, secure repeat business, and establish long-term partnerships. This section will explore communication best practices, handling difficult clients or conflicts, and building long-term client relationships.

4.3.1 Communication Best Practices

Clear and effective communication is the foundation of successful client relationships. Consider the following best practices:

1. Establish clear channels: Determine the primary modes of communication with your clients, such as

email, phone calls, or project management tools. Ensure that both you and the client are comfortable with these channels.

2. Set communication expectations: Agree with your clients on response times, availability, and preferred methods of communication. This helps manage their expectations and avoid unnecessary misunderstandings.

3. Be proactive in updates: Provide regular project updates to clients, even if there are no major milestones to report. This shows your commitment and keeps them informed of progress.

4. Practice active listening: Pay attention to your clients' needs and concerns. Repeat or summarize their statements to demonstrate understanding and ensure clarity.

5. Be concise and clear: Use clear and concise language in your communication to avoid misinterpretation. Break complex ideas into simple

terms and provide examples or visual aids when appropriate.

6. Document important conversations: Keep a record of important phone calls or in-person meetings by summarizing key points in writing and sending them to the client. This ensures everyone is on the same page and provides a reference for future discussions.

4.3.2 Dealing with Difficult Clients or Conflicts

Freelancers may encounter difficult clients or conflicts during their work. Here are some strategies for addressing these situations:

1. Stay calm and professional: When faced with challenging clients or conflicts, remain calm and composed. Respond in a professional manner, even if the client becomes confrontational.

2. Active listening and empathy: Practice active listening to understand the client's perspective and concerns. Show empathy and validate their feelings before offering potential solutions.

3. Address issues promptly: Deal with conflicts or problems as soon as they arise. Ignoring or delaying resolution can exacerbate the situation and damage the client relationship further.

4. Find common ground and compromise: Search for points of agreement and look for mutually beneficial solutions. Be open to compromise while still maintaining your professional boundaries.

5. Seek outside mediation if necessary: If conflicts persist and cannot be resolved directly with the client, consider involving a neutral third party or mediator to help facilitate discussions and find a resolution.

4.3.3 Building Long-Term Client Partnerships

Building long-term client partnerships is a valuable asset for freelancers. Consider the following tips to foster strong and lasting relationships:

1. Provide exceptional service: Deliver high-quality work, meet deadlines, and exceed client expectations whenever possible. Consistently delivering exceptional service builds trust and encourages clients to return.

2. Nurture ongoing communication: Maintain regular contact with clients, even after projects are completed. Send occasional updates, relevant industry articles, or personalized greetings to stay top-of-mind.

3. Offer additional value: Go above and beyond by providing additional insights or recommendations that can benefit the client's business. Offer suggestions for improvements or new opportunities whenever appropriate.

4. Ask for feedback: Regularly seek feedback from clients to gauge their satisfaction with your work and identify areas for improvement. Act on their feedback to continually enhance your services.

5. Show appreciation: Express gratitude for the opportunity to work with clients. Consider sending thank-you notes, small gifts, or discounts on future projects as gestures of appreciation.

6. Be proactive in maintaining relationships: Reach out to clients periodically, even when there are no immediate projects. Stay updated on their business needs and offer assistance or support when relevant.

By following these strategies, freelancers can effectively manage their client relationships, handle difficult situations with professionalism, and establish long-term partnerships that benefit both parties involved.

Chapter 5:

Balancing Work and Lifestyle as a Freelancer

5.1 Time Management and Productivity Techniques

As a freelancer, managing your time effectively and staying productive is essential to maintain a healthy work-life balance. This section covers key strategies to help you optimize your time and overcome common challenges such as setting realistic work schedules, utilizing time-tracking tools and apps, and combating procrastination.

5.1.1 Setting Realistic Work Schedules

Establishing realistic work schedules is vital for freelancers to maintain a steady workflow and avoid burnout. Consider the following tips:

1. Determine peak productivity hours: Identify the times of the day when you feel most energized and focused. Schedule your most critical and demanding tasks during these periods.

2. Set boundaries: Define specific working hours and communicate them to clients, friends, and family. Let others know when you are available and when you need uninterrupted work time.

3. Prioritize tasks: Create a to-do list or use task management tools to prioritize your tasks based on deadlines, importance, and urgency. Focus on completing high-priority items first.

4. Break down projects: Divide large projects into smaller, manageable tasks. This makes it easier to estimate the time required and allows for a more realistic schedule.

5. Allow for flexibility: While setting schedules, it's important to account for unexpected interruptions

or changes in client requirements. Leave some buffer time to handle unforeseen circumstances.

6. Take breaks: Incorporate regular breaks into your schedule to recharge and maintain focus. Short breaks can actually enhance productivity and prevent fatigue.

5.1.2 Utilizing Time-Tracking Tools and Apps

Time-tracking tools and apps can help freelancers monitor their work hours, measure productivity, and ensure accurate billing. Consider the following recommendations:

1. Choose a tool that suits your needs: Explore different time-tracking tools available and select one that aligns with your workflow and preferences. Look for features like timers, project categorization, and detailed reporting.

2. Track time diligently: Make it a habit to track your work hours accurately. Begin and end time tracking when you start and finish tasks, ensuring precise record-keeping.

3. Categorize and analyze your time: Use tags or categories to organize your time entries based on projects, clients, or tasks. This enables you to analyze how you spend your time and identify areas for improvement.

4. Review and assess productivity: Regularly review your time reports to evaluate your productivity levels. Assess how efficiently you are utilizing your working hours and make adjustments as necessary.

5. Automate time-tracking: Consider using automated time-tracking tools that can record your work time in the background while you focus on your tasks. This reduces the need for manual input and improves accuracy.

5.1.3 Overcoming Procrastination and Staying Focused

Procrastination can be a major challenge for freelancers. To combat it and stay focused, try the following techniques:

1. Break tasks into smaller steps: Large or overwhelming tasks can lead to procrastination. Break them down into smaller, more manageable steps to make them less daunting.

2. Set deadlines and milestones: Assign deadlines for individual tasks and establish milestones for larger projects. This creates a sense of urgency and helps maintain focus.

3. Eliminate distractions: Identify and minimize any potential distractions in your work environment. Turn off notifications, close unnecessary browser tabs, and create a dedicated workspace free from interruptions.

4. Use time-blocking techniques: Allocate specific time blocks for different tasks or types of work. This helps create structure and minimizes the temptation to switch between unrelated tasks.

5. Practice time management techniques: Explore productivity methods such as the Pomodoro Technique, where you work in focused sprints with short breaks in between. Experiment to find the techniques that work best for you.

6. Find accountability partners: Share your goals and progress with someone who can help hold you accountable. This can be a fellow freelancer, mentor, or friend who understands your

5.2 Financial Planning and Budgeting

As a freelancer, managing your finances is crucial for maintaining stability and achieving long-term financial security. This section highlights key strategies to help you effectively handle your irregular income streams, set financial goals, plan for taxes, and create an emergency fund.

5.2.1 Managing Irregular Income Streams

Freelancers often face the challenge of irregular income, which requires careful planning and budgeting. Consider the following tips:

1. Budget based on average income: Calculate your average income over the past several months or years. Use this figure as a baseline for budgeting your expenses and saving goals.

2. Separate business and personal finances: Open a separate business bank account to manage your freelance income and expenses. This helps you track your business finances accurately and simplifies tax preparation.

3. Build an emergency fund: Set aside a portion of your income to establish an emergency fund. Aim to

save three to six months' worth of living expenses to provide a financial cushion during lean periods.

4. Diversify your client base: Relying on a few clients for the majority of your income can be risky. Work towards diversifying your client base to mitigate the impact of potential client loss or fluctuations in demand.

5. Monitor cash flow: Keep a close eye on your cash flow by tracking incoming and outgoing payments. This helps you anticipate any shortfalls and make adjustments accordingly.

5.2.2 Setting Financial Goals and Saving for the Future

Setting financial goals is essential for freelancers to work towards a secure and fulfilling future. Consider the following strategies:

1. Define short-term and long-term goals: Identify your financial priorities and set clear goals for the short term *(e.g., paying off debt)* and the long term *(e.g., saving for retirement or purchasing a home).*

2. Establish a budget: Create a budget that factors in your income, expenses, and savings goals. Allocate a portion of your income towards savings and track your progress regularly.

3. Automate savings: Set up automatic transfers to your savings account to ensure consistent contributions towards your goals. This removes the temptation to spend money before saving.

4. Invest for the future: Consider investing a portion of your income in retirement accounts, stocks, mutual funds, or other investment vehicles. Consult a financial advisor to determine the best investment options for your situation.

5. Review and adjust goals periodically: Regularly assess your financial goals and adjust them as needed. Changes in income, market conditions, or personal circumstances may necessitate modifications to your savings and investment strategy.

5.2.3 Planning for Taxes and Creating an Emergency Fund

Managing taxes and creating an emergency fund are essential components of financial planning for freelancers. Consider the following tips:

1. Consult a tax professional: Seek guidance from a tax professional or accountant to understand your tax obligations as a freelancer. They can help you navigate tax regulations, track deductible expenses, and plan for quarterly tax payments.

2. Keep detailed records: Maintain organized and accurate records of your income, expenses, and receipts. This simplifies the tax filing process and

ensures that you take advantage of all eligible deductions.

3. Set aside funds for taxes: Allocate a portion of your income towards paying taxes. Set up a separate savings account specifically for tax payments and regularly contribute to it throughout the year.

4. Plan for an emergency fund: As mentioned previously, establish an emergency fund to cover unexpected expenses or periods of low income. This fund should be separate from your tax savings and easily accessible in case of emergencies.

5. Regularly review and adjust: Review your tax strategy and emergency fund periodically to ensure they align with your current financial situation. As your income and expenses change, make appropriate adjustments to optimize your financial planning.

By implementing these financial planning and budgeting strategies, freelancers can achieve greater stability, effectively manage their income, and safeguard their financial future.

5.3 Self-Care and Avoiding Burnout

Maintaining work-life balance, employing effective stress management techniques, and developing healthy habits and routines are essential for self-care and avoiding burnout. Let's explore these concepts and their biblical references, along with a personal testimony.

1. Maintaining work-life balance:

Maintaining a work-life balance means finding a healthy equilibrium between your professional and personal life. It involves setting boundaries and prioritizing rest and rejuvenation.

Biblical Reference: In **Mark 6:31,** Jesus says to his disciples, *"Come with me by yourselves to a quiet place and get some rest."* This shows the importance that Jesus placed on taking time for rest and rejuvenation.

Personal Testimony:

As a freelancer, I have faced the challenge of overworking and neglecting my personal life. However, I have learned to establish clear boundaries by allocating specified working hours and setting aside time for leisure activities and spending quality time with my loved ones. This has improved my work-life balance and brought me peace and fulfillment.

2. Effective stress management techniques:

Stress is a common experience for freelancers, but it's crucial to employ effective techniques to manage it. Practicing mindfulness, prayer, and self-care are powerful tools to combat stress.

Biblical Reference: **Philippians 4:6-7** says, "Do not be anxious about anything, but in every situation, by prayer and petition, with thanksgiving, present your requests to God. And the peace of God, which transcends all understanding, will guard your hearts and your minds in Christ Jesus." This verse reminds us to bring our worries to God through prayer and experience His peace.

Personal Testimony:

When I feel overwhelmed and stressed, I turn to prayer and mindfulness. I take a few moments to breathe deeply, reflect on God's goodness, and offer my concerns to Him. This practice helps me calm my mind, gain perspective, and experience a sense of peace that transcends the stressors of my work.

3. Developing healthy habits and routines:

Developing healthy habits and routines is essential for self-care. Prioritizing sleep, exercise, healthy eating, and setting a consistent routine can boost energy, productivity, and overall well-being.

Biblical Reference: In *1 Corinthians 10:31,* it says, *"So whether you eat or drink or whatever you do, do it all for the glory of God."* This verse reminds us to take care of our bodies as temples of the Holy Spirit, including nourishing them with healthy habits.

Personal Testimony:

I have made it a priority to establish healthy habits and routines. I prioritize getting enough sleep, engaging in regular exercise, and nourishing my body with nutritious foods. Additionally, setting a consistent routine helps me maintain discipline and structure in my work and personal life.

In conclusion, self-care and avoiding burnout as a freelancer involve maintaining work-life balance, employing effective stress management techniques, and developing healthy habits and routines. By implementing these strategies and drawing inspiration from biblical principles, we can find fulfillment, peace, and longevity in our freelancing journey.

Conclusion:

As we come to the end of The Ultimate 101 Guide to Freelancing, it's important to take a moment to reflect on the journey that lies behind and ahead. Freelancing is a dynamic and ever-evolving field, and your decision to embark on this path is a testament to your courage, creativity, and ambition.

Throughout this book, we have covered the essential aspects of freelancing, from understanding the freelance landscape and building a strong foundation to marketing yourself, managing clients, and taking care of your well-being. We have explored the importance of embracing flexibility, cultivating a growth mindset, and seizing opportunities for personal and professional development.

Remember, freelancing is not always without its challenges. The road may be filled with uncertainty, competition, and setbacks. However, with determination, perseverance, and the knowledge gained from this guide, you are equipped to overcome these challenges and achieve your goals.

As you navigate your freelancing journey, it is important to stay open to learning and growth. Embrace feedback, seek mentorship, and continuously refine your skills. Keep an eye on emerging trends and adapt to the evolving needs of clients and the market.

In addition to the practical strategies and guidance shared in this book, it is also crucial to cultivate a mindset of faith, courage, and gratitude. Rely on your faith as a source of strength and inspiration, knowing that you have a divine purpose and are equipped with unique gifts and talents. Lean on the support of your friends, family, and fellow freelancers, as their encouragement can uplift you during challenging times.

Lastly, remember to celebrate your successes, big and small. Freelancing offers ample opportunities for personal fulfillment and growth. Take a moment to acknowledge and appreciate your achievements, as they are the stepping stones to even greater heights.

As you continue your freelancing journey, there are many resources and further reading materials available to deepen your knowledge and expand your skill set. Stay curious, explore new concepts, and engage with communities of freelancers who can offer support and insights. Some suggested resources and reading materials are:

- "The Freelancer's Bible" by Sara Horowitz

- "The 4 Hour Workweek" by Timothy Ferriss

- "The $100 Startup" by Chris Guillebeau

- Online communities and forums such as Freelancers Union and Upwork Community.

In conclusion, I want to express my gratitude for joining me on this freelancing adventure. I hope this book has provided you with valuable insights, practical strategies, and inspiration to thrive as a freelancer. Embrace the freedom, creativity, and personal fulfillment that freelancing offers, and remember that your skills and passions have the power to shape a successful and fulfilling career on your own terms.

Wishing you all the best on your continued journey as a freelancer!

Prophet PD John

www.ingramcontent.com/pod-product-compliance
Lightning Source LLC
Chambersburg PA
CBHW071944210526
45479CB00002B/804